HAVE A MOTHER, TOO ?

by Eric Carle

Collins

An imprint of HarperCollinsPublishers

YES!

A **KANGAROO** has a mother.
Just like me and you.

Does a lion have a mother, too?

Yes!
A **LION** has a mother.
Just like me and you.

Does a giraffe have a mother, too?

Yes!
A GIRAFFE has a mother.
Just like me and you.

Does a penguin have a mother, too?

Yes!
A **PENGUIN** has a mother.
Just like me and you.

Does a swan have a mother, too?

Yes!
A SWAN has a mother.
Just like me and you.

Does a fox have a mother, too?

Yes!
A **FOX** has a mother.
Just like me and you.

Does a dolphin have a mother, too?

Yes!
A **DOLPHIN** has a mother.
Just like me and you.

Does a sheep have a mother, too?

Yes!
A **SHEEP** has a mother.
Just like me and you.

Does a bear have a mother, too?

Yes!
A **BEAR** has a mother.
Just like me and you.

Does an elephant have a mother, too?

Yes!
An **ELEPHANT** has a mother.
Just like me and you.

Does a monkey have a mother, too?

Yes!
A **MONKEY** has a mother.
Just like me and you.

And do animal mothers love their babies?

YES ! YES ! Of course they do.

*Animal mothers love their babies,
just as yours loves you.*

Names of animal babies, parents, and groups in this book

Kangaroo A baby kangaroo is a *joey*. Its mother is a *flyer* and its father is a *boomer*. A group of kangaroos is a *troop* or a *mob* or a *herd*.

Lion A baby lion is a *cub*. Its mother is a *lioness* and its father is a *lion*. A group of lions is a *pride*.

Giraffe A baby giraffe is a *calf*. Its mother is a *cow* and its father is a *bull*. A group of giraffes is a *tower* or a *herd*.

Penguin A baby penguin is a *chick*. Its mother is a *dam* and its father is a *sire*. A group of penguins is a *colony* or a *parade*.

Swan A baby swan is a *cygnet*. Its mother is a *pen* and its father is a *cob*. A group of swans is a *wedge* or a *herd*.

Fox A baby fox is a *cub* or a *pup*. Its mother is a *vixen* and its father is a *dog fox*. A group of foxes is a *pack* or a *skulk*.

Dolphin A baby dolphin is a *calf*. Its mother is a *cow* and its father is a *bull*. A group of dolphins is a *school* or a *pod*.

Sheep A baby sheep is a *lamb*. Its mother is a *ewe* and its father is a *ram*. A group of sheep is a *flock*.

Bear A baby bear is a *cub*. Its mother is a *sow* and its father is a *boar*. A group of bears is a *pack* or a *sloth*.

Elephant A baby elephant is a *calf*. Its mother is a *cow* and its father is a *bull*. A group of elephants is a *herd*.

Monkey A baby monkey is an *infant*. Its mother is a *mother* and its father is a *father*. A group of monkeys is a *group* or a *troop* or a *tribe*.

Deer A baby deer is a *fawn*. Its mother is a *doe* and its father is a *buck*. A group of deer is a *herd*.

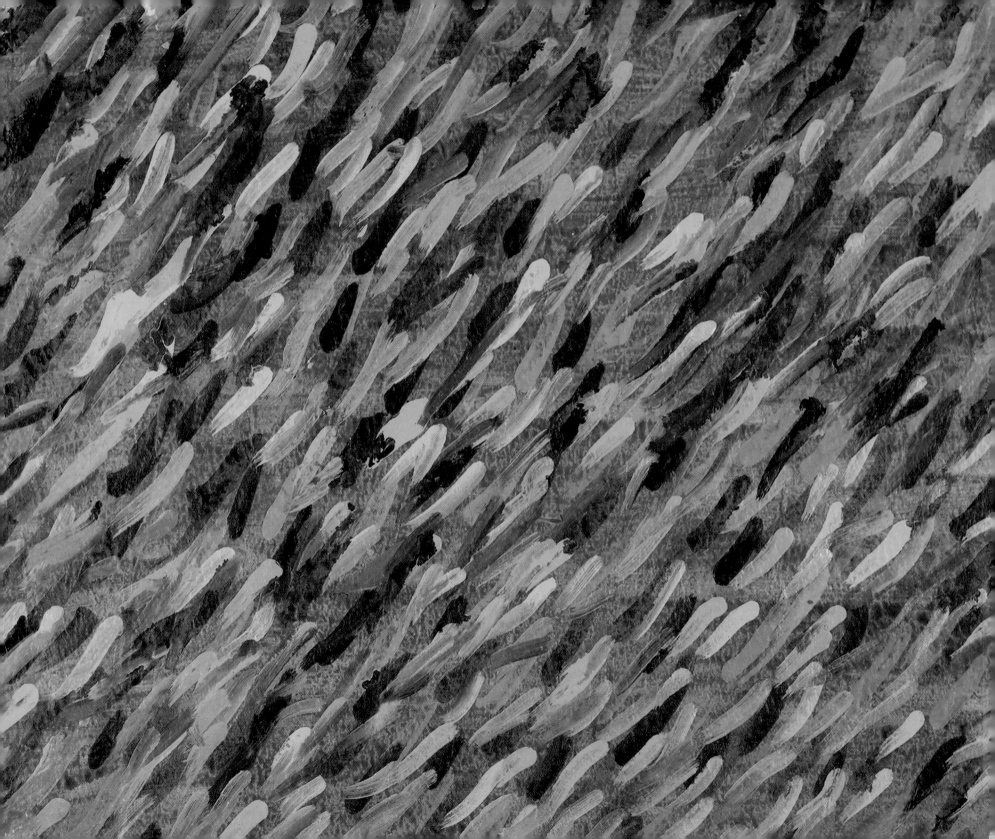